PIANO • VOCAL • GUITAR

SONGS OF THE 40's

THE DECADE SERIES

HAL•LEONARD™
CORPORATION
7777 W. BLUEMOUND RD. P.O. BOX 13819 MILWAUKEE, WI 53213

SONGS OF THE 40's
THE DECADE SERIES

Contents

The Forties

by Stanley Green

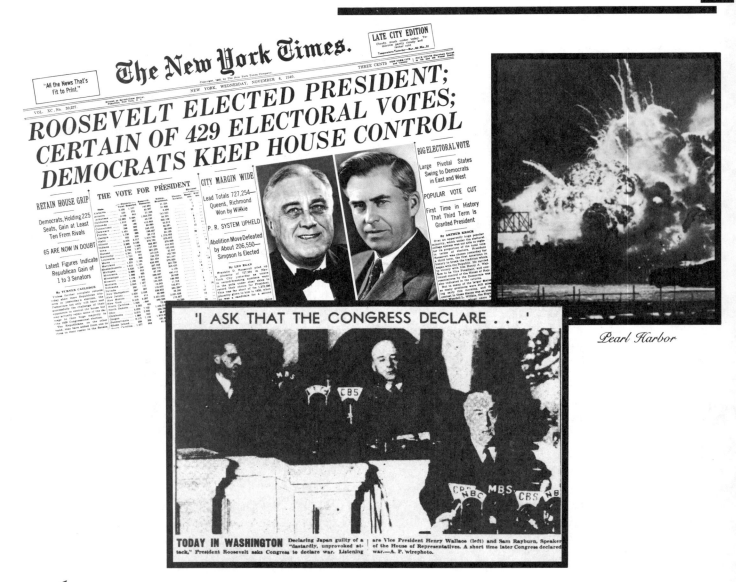

Pearl Harbor

$\mathcal{A}$t first they called it the Phony War, when it seemed as if the French and German armies would be forever stalemated on opposite sides of the Maginot Line. But four months into the new decade, the Second World War erupted in all its fury with a staggering succession of pulverizing Nazi blitzkriegs. Denmark fell in four hours. Norway in thirty-two days. Holland in five days. Belgium in eighteen. After seven of Hitler's columns pushed their way into France, the best that British and French forces could do was to escape annihilation through their heroic rescue at Dunkirk. With Italy now in the war on the side of its Axis partner, France was forced into a humiliating surrender in a railroad carriage in the forest of Compiegne. British Prime Minister Winston Churchill rallied his island kingdom by offering nothing more than "blood, toil, tears, and sweat," as night after night the Luftwaffe bombarded the major cities of England. Then, inevitably, the war spread to eastern Europe when the tenuous alliance between Hitler and Stalin was shattered by Germany's invasion of the Soviet Union.

On this side of the Atlantic, President Franklin D. Roosevelt, now serving an unprecedented third term, declared an unlimited state of national emergency, arranged a lend-lease program to aid the beleaguered Allies, proclaimed the United States "the arsenal of democracy," and joined with Churchill in spelling out their peace aims in the Atlantic Charter. Nothing, however, could control events or stem the spreading carnage. On December 7, 1941 — a date, Roosevelt said, "which will live in infamy" — the Japanese struck at Pearl Harbor and the United States was at last officially in the conflict.

Harry S. Truman

It wasn't long before Americans became familiar with the names of faraway places that only a few had ever heard of before — Bataan and Corregidor in the Philippines where Gen. Douglas MacArthur's men were forced to surrender...Sevastopol, where Russian defenders held out against the German juggernaut for eight months...

Iwo Jima

Lidice, Czechoslovakia, where Nazis slaughtered an entire village...El Alamein and Tobruk, where British victories turned the tide against Field Marshal Erwin Rommel's Afrika Korps... Guadalcanel, the first Japanese island to be recaptured by American forces...Anzio, on the western Italian coast, where U.S. and British troops made their initial landings in Europe...Auschwitz, where 476,000 Hungarian Jews were sent to their death...Omaha Beach on the French Normandy coastline where, on "D-Day," Gen. Dwight D. Eisenhower's liberating armies met their fiercest resistance... Tacloban on the island of Leyte, where MacArthur waded ashore to begin the liberation of the Philippines...Iwo Jima, where Yanks wrested control from the Japanese and raised the stars and stripes atop Mt. Suribachi...Hiroshima and Nagasaki, where President Harry S. Truman, Roosevelt's successor, made the fateful decision to drop the atom bomb that brought the war to an end.

Like most wars, World War II produced its share of patriotic, inspirational, sentimental, and comic songs that still evoke memories of those tragic and courageous times. From England, "A Nightingale Sang in Berkeley Square" offered a measure of hope during the dark days of the Battle of Britain; "The Last Time I Saw Paris" was Jerome Kern and Oscar Hammerstein's tender recollection of the charms of the French capital in the days before the Nazi occupation; the haunting "Lili Marlene," though a German song, was soon adopted by British and American forces in North Africa; and "Saturday Night Is the Loneliest Night in the Week" was the lament of frustrated young women everywhere who were compelled to spend their weekends alone while their loved ones were serving their country.

Once the war was finally over, the leaders of this ravaged planet set about the difficult task of searching for ways to establish a lasting peace. In the summer of 1945, representatives of 46 nations met in San Francisco to sign the charter of the United Nations. Nazi war criminals were brought to justice at the Nuremberg trials. And the Marshall Plan — named for its sponsor, Secretary of State George C. Marshall — was approved by Congress to help rehabilitate the countries of Europe and Asia.

Other major events, both shocking and dramatic, were also occurring in the United States during the post-war years. The French liner Normandie burned and sank while tied up in New York harbor. In Boston, 491 people perished in the Cocoanut Grove fire. The House Un-American Activities Committee set up shop to ferret out Communists, and Whittaker Chambers accused State Department aide Alger Hiss of being a Soviet spy. The Forties also saw the biggest political upset in American history when Truman confounded the pollsters by beating Gov. Thomas E. Dewey in the Presidential election. For diversion from matters of state and weight, the "New Look" was emphasizing longer, fuller skirts; canasta became the latest card-game craze; people actually claimed to see flying saucers in the sky; and changes in home entertainment were being caused by two important developments — the boom in the popularity of television and the invention of the long-playing record.

V-J Day Parade

When the decade began, dance orchestras were still providing the chief means through which song hits were being made. The main difference was that the beat had slowed down noticeably since the heyday of the swing bands. Thus Sammy Kaye's Swing and Sway boys were more likely to sway than to swing such numbers as "The Old Lamplighter" and "Daddy." Harry James' luminous horn took on a mellower tone as it led the band in "I'm Beginning to See the Light" (co-composed by James and Duke Ellington). And Glenn Miller's orchestra was suitably ethereal as it brought back memories of "Polka Dots and Moonbeams." Occasionally, though, a jazzier, more uptempo beat would break through, notably in Miller's "Tuxedo Junction," Tommy Dorsey's "Opus One," and both Miller's and Benny Goodman's versions of "A String of Pearls."

One special sound that won favor throughout the Forties was that of Latin and Latin-type music. "The Breeze and I" was adapted from Cuban composer Ernesto Lecuona's "Andalucia, Suite Española" to become a hit single for Tommy Dorsey's older brother Jimmy, who also had success with the Spanish "Amapola." And another Cuban number, "Poinciana," became a top selling record in its lush treatment by David Rose and his Orchestra.

Frank Sinatra

The Andrews Sisters

But it was becoming abundantly clear that the days of the mass popularity of big bands were numbered. Not only did wartime travel restrictions make it difficult for them to tour the country, the drafting of many musicians into the services helped bring about a sharp reduction in available personnel. Even in the early Forties, their place in the musical spotlight was being shared by the vocalists — whether singly or in groups — who would become the dominant attraction by the decade's end. During the war years, no performers were more closely identified with the music of the period than the harmonizing Andrews Sisters. One of their catchiest hits, "Boogie Woogie Bugle Boy," even managed to combine the sound of boogie woogie (a rumbling figured-bass pattern associated with honky-tonk pianos) with an up-to-date lyric about an irrepressible GI bugler.

Looming even larger on the musical scene was a hollow-cheeked, ex-band singer named Frank Sinatra who, in 1943, caused 30,000 bobby soxers to riot in the streets during an engagement at New York's Paramount Theatre. Also attracting loyal fans were such singing sensations of the decade as Ella Fitzgerald ("Imagination"), the Mills Brothers ("I Don't Want to Set the World on Fire," "I'll Be Around," "Across the Alley from the Alamo"), Jo Stafford ("Candy"), Nat "King" Cole ("For Sentimental Reasons"), Dinah Shore ("Shoo-Fly Pie and Apple Pan Dowdy"), and Vaughn Monroe ("Ballerina").

"Pal Joey"

"Oklahoma!"

Rodgers & Hammerstein

"One Touch Of Venus"
Starring Mary Martin

"Kiss Me, Kate"

On Broadway, Richard Rodgers was acknowledged as the decade's most influential composer. With his first partner, lyricist Lorenz Hart, he wrote the score for the hard-edged, cynical *Pal Joey,* which gave Vivienne Segal the chance to sing "Bewitched" and Gene Kelly the chance to sing "I Could Write a Book." In 1943, Rodgers teamed with a new lyricist, Oscar Hammerstein II, to inaugurate a different form of musical theatre with their seminal production, *Oklahoma!* "Oh, What A Beautiful Mornin'," "People Will Say We're in Love," "The Surrey With the Fringe on Top," and "Oklahoma" were four of the standards in this landmark score, while "June Is Bustin' Out All Over" and "You'll Never Walk Alone" were among the gems in the second Rodgers and Hammerstein stage work, *Carousel.*

Other writers who graced Broadway with their songs were Harold Arlen and Johnny Mercer with *St. Louis Woman* ("Come Rain or Come Shine"), Burton Lane and E. Y. Harburg with *Finian's Rainbow* ("How Are Things in Glocca Morra?," "Old Devil Moon"), Cole Porter with his biggest hit, *Kiss Me, Kate* ("So in Love," "Wunderbar"), and Kurt Weill and Ogden Nash with *One Touch of Venus* ("Speak Low"), starring Mary Martin.

*M*otion pictures of the Forties also provided their share of musical pleasures. "When You Wish Upon a Star" (sung on the soundtrack by Cliff Edwards) was heard in Walt Disney's second full-length animated cartoon, *Pinocchio;* the canorous "I'll Remember April" turned up in — of all places — Abbott and Costello's *Ride 'Em, Cowboy;* and "You'd Be So Nice to Come Home To," by Cole Porter, was introduced in a long-forgotten movie called *Something to Shout About.* During the decade Bing Crosby maintained his position as the screen's number-one singing actor, appearing in twenty-two films including *Going My Way* ("Swinging on a Star") and *Road to Rio* ("But Beautiful"), the fifth of Crosby's seven "Road" shows with Bob Hope and Dorothy Lamour. Following their Broadway triumph *Oklahoma!,* Rodgers and Hammerstein contributed the songs to *State Fair,* another slice of rural Americana in which the swooping waltz "It's a Grand Night for Singing" was first sung. Al Jolson, once billed as "The World's Greatest Entertainer," enjoyed a comeback in the mid-Forties when his dubbed voice was heard coming out of the mouth of Larry Parks in *The Jolson Story.* Though the songs consisted of old favorites, there was one "new" ballad, "Anniversary Song," whose melody dated back sixty years to a Rumanian composition known as "Danube Waves." Also of foreign origin was Anton Karas's ominous, jangling theme from *The Third Man,* which was performed by the composer on a zither as background music for a drama of East-West espionage set in post-war Vienna.

*O*f course, people didn't need movies to remind them that international tensions still remained high in 1949. Still, there was some comfort to be derived from the fact that the decade ended not with a whimper (as did the Twenties), nor with a bang (as did the Thirties), but with an audible sigh of relief that no world-wide catastrophe seemed to be looming in the imminent future.

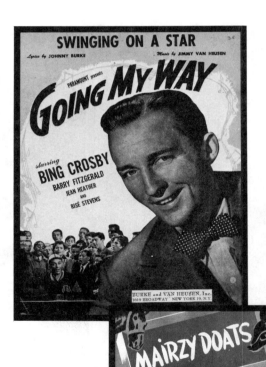

World Leaders

Franklin D. Roosevelt

Josef Stalin

Winston Churchill

Gen. Dwight D. Eisenhower

Gen. Douglas MacArthur

ACROSS THE ALLEY FROM THE ALAMO

Words and Music by JOE GREENE

ANNIVERSARY SONG

By AL JOLSON
and SAUL CHAPLIN

AMAPOLA
(PRETTY LITTLE POPPY)

By JOSEPH M. LACALLE
New English Words by ALBERT GAMSE

BEWITCHED
(From "PAL JOEY")

Words by LORENZ HART
Music by RICHARD RODGERS

Moderately, in 2

mf

He's a fool and don't I know it. But a fool can have his charms.
Love's the same old sad sen-sa-tion. Late-ly I've not slept a wink

I'm in love and don't I show it, Like a babe in arms.
Since this half-pint im-i-ta-tion

Put me on the blink. I'm wild a-gain, Be-guiled a-gain, A

BUT BEAUTIFUL

Words and Music by JOHNNY BURKE
and JAMES VAN HEUSEN

24

BLUEBERRY HILL

Words and Music by
AL LEWIS, LARRY STOCK and VINCENT ROSE

BOOGIE WOOGIE BUGLE BOY

Words and Music by DON RICE
and HUGHIE PRINCE

Medium Boogie Woogie

He was a fa - mous trum - pet man from out Chi -

ca - go way, ___ He had a "boo - gie" style that no one

else could play. ___ He was the top man of his craft

MCA MUSIC

31

THE BREEZE AND I

Words by AL STILLMAN
Music by ERNESTO LECUONA

CANDY

Words and Music by MACK DAVID,
JOAN WHITNEY and ALEX KRAMER

Moderately slow

COME RAIN OR COME SHINE

(From "ST. LOUIS WOMAN")

Words by JOHNNY MERCER
Music by HAROLD ARLEN

CRUISING DOWN THE RIVER

Words and Music by
EILY BEADELL and NELL TOLLERTON

39

(I Love You)
FOR SENTIMENTAL REASONS

Words by DEEK WATSON
Music by WILLIAM BEST

MCA MUSIC PUBLISHING

43

DADDY

Words and Music by
Bob Troup

Medium bounce tempo

VOICE

Hey! lis - ten to my sto - ry 'bout_ a

gal named Dai - sy Mae_ La - zy Dai - sy Mae_

Her dis-po - si - tion   is ra-ther sweet and charm-ing;

At times a - larm - ing.   So_ they say. _____

(Interlude)

She had a

man rich, tall, dark, hand-some   large and strong to whom she used to sing this song:

46

GOD BLESS' THE CHILD

Words and Music by ARTHUR HERZOG, JR.
and BILLIE HOLIDAY

HARLEM NOCTURNE

Words by DICK ROGERS
Music by EARLE HAGEN

HOW ARE THINGS
IN GLOCCA MORRA

(From "FINIAN'S RAINBOW")

Words by E.Y. HARBURG
Music by BURTON LANE

HAVE I TOLD YOU LATELY THAT I LOVE YOU

Words and Music by SCOTT WISEMAN

MCA MUSIC

HOW HIGH THE MOON
(From "TWO FOR THE SHOW")

Words by NANCY HAMILTON
Music by MORGAN LEWIS

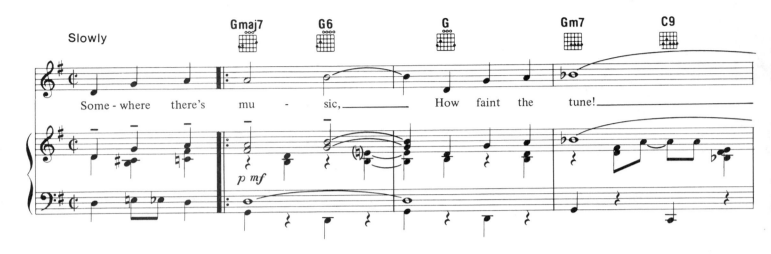

Slowly

Some-where there's mu - sic,_____ How faint the tune!_____

Some-where there's heav - en,_____ How High The Moon!_____ There is no

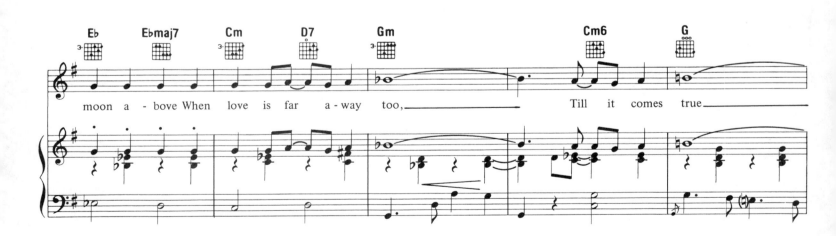

moon a - bove When love is far a - way too,_____ Till it comes true_____

I COULD WRITE A BOOK

(From "PAL JOEY")

Words by LORENZ HART
Music by RICHARD RODGERS

I DON'T WANT TO SET THE WORLD ON FIRE

Words by EDDIE SEILER and SOL MARCUS
Music by BENNIE BENJAMIN and EDDIE DURHAM

I'LL BE AROUND

Words and Music by
ALEC WILDER

I'LL REMEMBER APRIL

Words and Music by
DON RAYE, GENE DePAUL
and PAT JOHNSON

I'M BEGINNING TO SEE THE LIGHT

Words and Music by HARRY JAMES,
DUKE ELLINGTON, JOHNNY HODGES
and DON GEORGE

8vb

IMAGINATION

Words by JOHNNY BURKE
Music by JIMMY VAN HEUSEN

IT'S A GRAND NIGHT FOR SINGING
(From "STATE FAIR")

Bright Waltz

Words by OSCAR HAMMERSTEIN II
Music by RICHARD RODGERS

IT'S A MOST UNUSUAL DAY

Words by HAROLD ADAMSON
Music by JIMMY McHUGH

JUKE BOX SATURDAY NIGHT

Words by Al Stillman
Music by Paul McGrane

JUNE IS BUSTIN' OUT ALL OVER

Words by OSCAR HAMMERSTEIN II
Music by RICHARD RODGERS

THE LAST TIME I SAW PARIS

Words by OSCAR HAMMERSTEIN II
Music by JEROME KERN

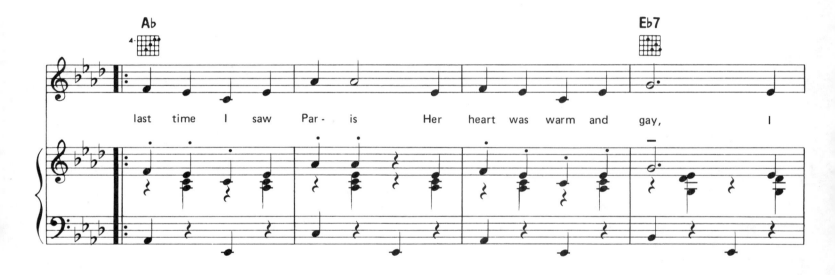

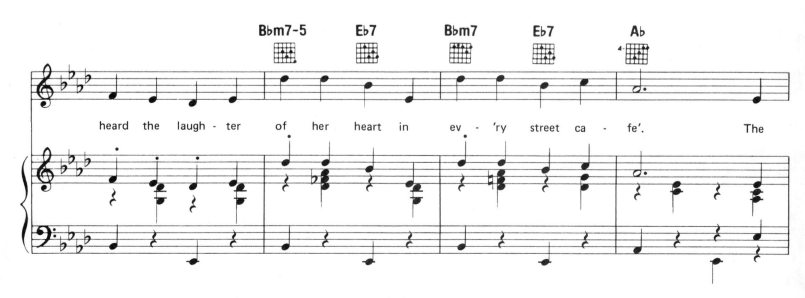

LILLI MARLENE

German Lyric by HANS LEIP
English Lyric by TOMMIE CONNOR
Music by NORBERT SCHULTZE

Slowly

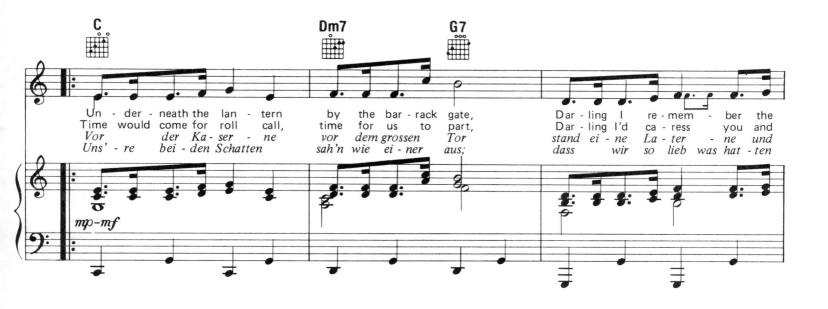

Un - der - neath the lan - tern by the bar - rack gate,
Time would come for roll call, time for us to part,
Vor der Ka - ser - ne vor dem grossen Tor
Uns' - re bei - den Schatten sah'n wie ei - ner aus;

Dar - ling I re - mem - ber the
Dar - ling I'd ca - ress you and
stand ei - ne La - ter - ne und
dass wir so lieb was hat - ten

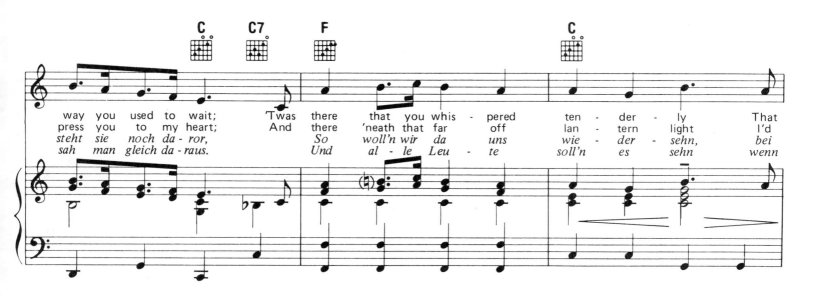

way you used to wait; 'Twas there that you whis - pered ten - der - ly
press you to my heart; And there 'neath that far off lan - tern light
steht sie noch da - ror, So woll'n wir da uns wie - der - sehn,
sah man gleich da - raus. Und al - le Leu - te soll'n es sehn

That
I'd
bei
wenn

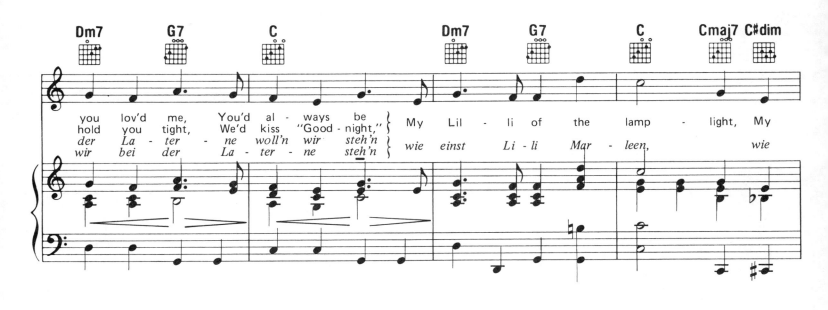

you lov'd me, You'd al - ways be

hold you tight, We'd kiss "Good - night," } My Lil - li of the lamp - light, My

der La - ter - ne woll'n wir steh'n

wir bei der La - ter - ne steh'n } *wie einst Li - li Mar - leen,* wie

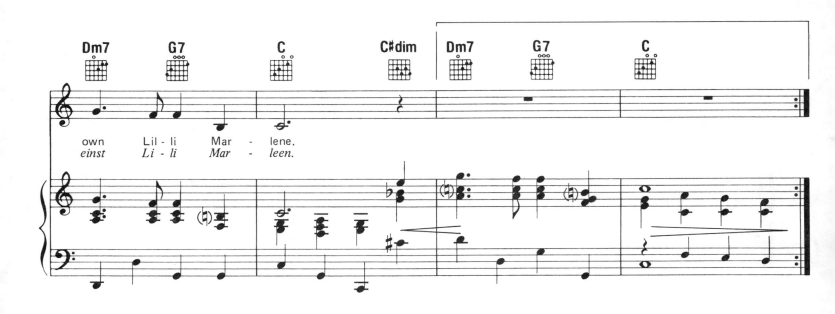

own Lil - li Mar - lene.

einst Li - li Mar - leen.

Or - ders came for sail - ing some - where o - ver there, All con - fined to bar - racks was

Rest - ing in A bill - et just be - hind the line, E - ven tho' we're part - ed your

Schon rief der Po - sten: sie bla - sen Za - pfen sheich; es kann drei Ta - ge ko - sten! Ka - me

Dei - ne Schrit - te kennt sie, dei - nen zie - ren Gang, al - le A - bend brennt sie

Aus dem stil - lin Rau - me, aus der Er - de Grund hebt mich wie im Trau - me

mf - f

MAIRZY DOATS

By MILTON DRAKE, AL HOFFMAN,
and JERRY LIVINGSTON

MANAGUA, NICARAGUA

Words by ALBERT GAMSE
Music by IRVING FIELDS

A NIGHTINGALE SANG IN BERKELEY SQUARE

Lyric by ERIC MASCHWITZ
Music by MANNING SHERWIN

MOONLIGHT IN VERMONT

Words and Music by JOHN BLACKBURN
and KARL SUESSDORF

105

OH, WHAT A BEAUTIFUL MORNIN'
(From "OKLAHOMA!")

Words by OSCAR HAMMERSTEIN II
Music by RICHARD RODGERS

107

OKLAHOMA
(From "OKLAHOMA!")

Words by OSCAR HAMMERSTEIN II
Music by RICHARD RODGERS

THE OLD LAMPLIGHTER

Words by Charles Tobias
Music by Nat Simon

OLD DEVIL MOON

(From "FINIAN'S RAINBOW")

Words by E. Y. HARBURG
Music by BURTON LANE

115

THE OLD SOFT SHOE

Words by Nancy Hamilton
Music by Morgan Lewis

OPUS ONE

Words and Music by
SY OLIVER and SID GARRIS

PEOPLE WILL SAY WE'RE IN LOVE

(From "OKLAHOMA!")

Words by OSCAR HAMMERSTEIN II
Music by RICHARD RODGERS

POINCIANA
(Song Of The Tree)

Words by BUDDY BERNIER
Music by NAT SIMON

POLKA DOTS AND MOONBEAMS

Words by JOHNNY BURKE
Music by JIMMY VAN HEUSEN

129

130

SATURDAY NIGHT IS THE LONELIEST NIGHT OF THE WEEK

Words by SAMMY CAHN
Music by JULE STYNE

RED ROSES FOR A BLUE LADY

By SID TEPPER
and ROY C. BENNETT

SEEMS LIKE OLD TIMES

Words and Music by Carmen Lombardo
and John Jacob Loeb

SHOO FLY PIE AND APPLE PAN DOWDY

Words by SAMMY GALLOP
Music by GUY WOOD

Slow bounce

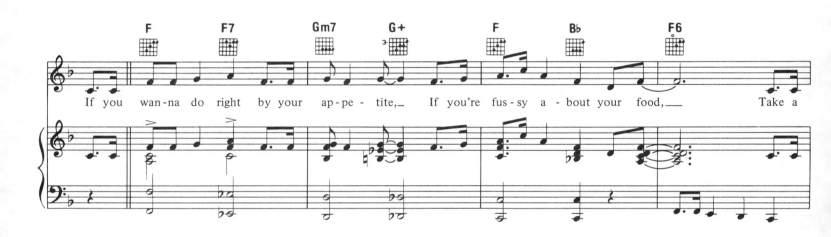

If you wan-na do right by your ap-pe-tite,_ If you're fus-sy a-bout your food,_ Take a

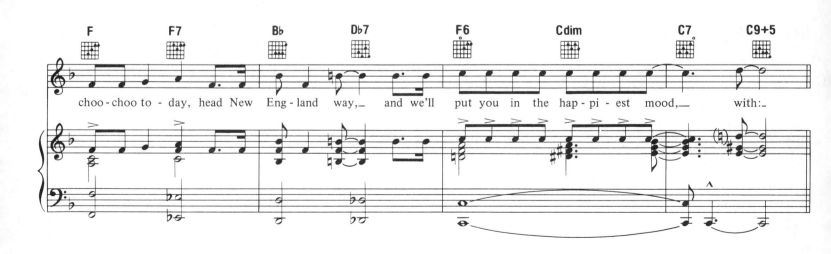

choo-choo to-day, head New Eng-land way,_ and we'll put you in the hap-pi-est mood,_ with:_

SPEAK LOW

(From "ONE TOUCH OF VENUS")

Words by OGDEN NASH
Music by KURT WEILL

SO IN LOVE
(From "KISS ME KATE")

Words and Music by COLE PORTER

A STRING OF PEARLS

Words by EDDIE DELANGE
Music by JERRY GRAY

Moderately Bright

A SUNDAY KIND OF LOVE

Words and Music by BARBARA BELLE,
LOUIS PRIMA, ANITA LEONARD and STAN RHODES

Moderately Slow

MCA MUSIC PUBLISHING

TUXEDO JUNCTION

Words by BUDDY FEYNE
Music by ERSKINE HAWKINS, WILLIAM JOHNSON
and JULIAN DASH

THE SURREY WITH THE FRINGE ON TOP

(From "OKLAHOMA!")

Words by OSCAR HAMMERSTEIN II
Music by RICHARD RODGERS

SWINGING ON A STAR

Words and Music by Johnny Burke and Jimmy Van Heusen

THERE MUST BE A WAY

Words and Music by SAMMY GALLOP
and DAVID SAXON

169

THE THINGS WE DID LAST SUMMER

Words and Music by SAMMY CAHN
and JULE STYNE

THE THIRD MAN THEME

Words by WALTER LORD
Based on music composed & arranged by ANTON KARAS

When a zith-er starts to play, You'll re-mem-ber yes - ter-day;

In its haunt-ing strain, Vi - en-na lives a-gain, Free and bright and gay.

In your mind__ a sud-den gleam of a half__ for-got-ten dream,

G7

hush _____ And in the morn-ing traf - fic rush _____ A

C   G7   D.S. al Coda

song that's al-ways new   In your heart, a _____ part   of you.   Oh,

CODA
G7

of   a   well _____ re - mem-bered dream   Shines so bright-ly when   you

cresc.

C

hear   The Third   Man   Theme. _____

sfz

WHEN YOU WISH UPON A STAR

(From Walt Disney's "PINOCCHIO")

Words by NED WASHINGTON
Music by LEIGH HARLINE

With expression

WUNDERBAR
(From "KISS ME, KATE")

Words and Music by COLE PORTER

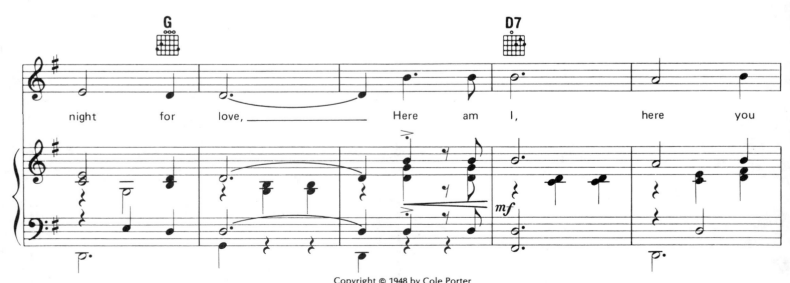

bar!_____ There's our fav'-rite star a-bove,_____ What a bright shin - ing star,_____ Like our love, it's wun - der - bar!_____ Wun - der - love, it's wun - der - bar!_____

YOU CAN'T BE TRUE DEAR
(Du Kannst Nicht Treu Sein)

English lyric by HAL COTTON
Original German text by GERHARD EBELER
Music by HANS OTTEN and KEN GRIFFIN

You can't be true, dear _____ There's noth - ing
more to say _____ I trust - ed you
dear Hop - ing we'd find a way _____

187

You'll Never Walk Alone

(From "CAROUSEL")

Words by OSCAR HAMMERSTEIN II
Music by RICHARD RODGERS

YOU'D BE SO NICE TO COME HOME TO
(From "SOMETHING TO SHOUT ABOUT")

Words and Music by COLE PORTER

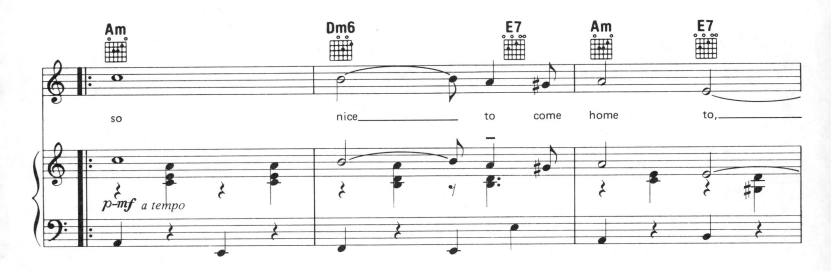